Rejuvenate

Your Life!

21 Days to Feel Like a Woman Again

Inez Bracy

The Bracy Group
http://InezBracy.com.

Contents

Rejuvenate Your Life

When you look at your life, what do you see? Do you see problems that need fixing, challenges that need addressing, opportunities to explore—or a mystery to unfold? Do you remember how "things used to be" when you had a definite aim for your life? Has your life gotten out of control because you allow others to define your purpose?

The way you view your life will determine your attitude about it. If everything tends to be a problem, or even an annoyance, that constantly needs fixing, you will stay in a state of chaos or crisis. This causes all types of health problems, such as, eating or drinking too much or too little, high blood pressure, overall fatigue, and a feeling of being incomplete of never finishing anything.

Imagine what your life would be like if you could recapture some of the thoughts and attitudes of your youth, the thoughts you had when you defined yourself and lived your life on purpose! When you live your "best life", life takes on new meaning. You develop and feel a new attitude of ease, knowing that you are in control of what you can be and in flow with what you can't.

Using your imagination as a focal point, begin to look at the issues that arise as a mystery to unfold, so that you can rejuvenate your life and live in a state of high expectations and enjoyment. This gives you an overall feeling of happiness and goodwill, a feeling of completeness, a feeling that you are on purpose and that things have been handled and are finished. Which will you choose?

Think about a small child exploring her world Each item she encounters is a marvel, to be picked up, and looked upon with great excitement and expectation. She turns it every way she can to get a grasp of what the item is. Once she has mastered it, she moves on to the next thing with the same excitement and expectation. This is the way she learns her world, it is a mystery to unfold.

You know your world; you've already turned things to see all facets. What would be the difference in your life if you could recapture that childlike attitude and joy? Regaining that perspective is possible if you are willing to let go of the baggage, (old hurts, disappointments, losses, emotional ties and attachments, and etc) which keeps you stuck and the absence of which will allow you to embrace your change.

At this point, you could be thinking "but this is what I know" and "what if the new attitude doesn't work?" The real question is: "Is the old attitude working; is living in chaos and crisis working?"

Has a particular negative habit become so entrenched that you don't want to get rid of it? A habit is something that you have become accustom to having or doing. Habits form from thoughts and actions. Habits happen because you do the same thing over and over until you do it without thinking about it. Sometimes this is healthy, as habits make our world more understandable. However, some habits acquired over many years are causing pain or is making you uncomfortable. You wish you could quit the habit but are unable to quit. Sometimes you quit for a day or a week but rarely make it longer.

During that transition time, you will likely experience a delayed sense of shock at what you were putting up with, and then, ideally, experience a state of authentic being. This is where rejuvenation starts to be felt. Living in an authentic state of being is not the same as having or doing—being is transcending the physical and living on a higher plane. Being is living as if you already have the desires of your heart. This is not implying that one lives a lie or in an unreal state on a daily basis; being is as if one is breathing regardless of how life is unfolding.

Research shows that it takes twenty-one (21) days to form a habit; therefore it is a good idea to plan to take twenty-one (21) days to replace a given habit. Habits have considerable effect habit on your daily life, from helping you "get through" the day to keeping you in crisis patterns to giving positive order to your life.

In beginning to shift undesirable habits, you must commit to a twenty-one day program. You may think you don't have that much time, or that real life is like the

21-minute sitcom (minus the commercials) in our instant society, or that gratification should come faster if you really want it. However, it is vital to remember that twenty-one days will come whether you follow the program or not. Wouldn't it be nice to be celebrating your successes twenty-one days from now rather than lamenting that it will take twenty-one days once you finally start?

The best way to get rid of a habit is to replace it with a new habit. Now that you know how a little more about how a habit is formed, let's look at replacing a particular undesirable habit with a "just being your best" habit. This program requires that you release negative habits, change some habits and make new habits.

One of the habits that you will form is to spend a few minutes in reflection each day, completing the exercises for that day. This is to keep you grounded, centered and on track for the next day, incorporating your discoveries into your inner knowingness. Using this rejuvenation technique will let you know where you have been, how far you have come and where you are going. As part of the reflection process you are encouraged to journal your thoughts at the end of the day. It doesn't have to be fancy—it can be a notebook or a leather bound tome. Whatever works for you, because this is a written record for your eyes only! Remember, there is no penalty for not writing, but it will only affect you if you don't do the work.

Your Journey Begins NOW!

How do you go from where you are to where you want to be? I think you have to have an enthusiasm for life. You have to have a dream, a goal and you have to be willing to work for it.

~ Jim Valvano

Think of a time of ecstatic engagement, a time when all was going "your way" and you felt on top of the world. Ecstatic engagement feels like joy and excitement infuse your entire body, that the air is clearer, colors are brighter... all is absolutely right with your world.

Your time of ecstatic engagement might be a wedding, birth of a child, receiving a degree, returning to school... just remember the feeling you got at that time.

Why is this important? Because you get to create this feeling as often as you like any time you like. Remembering this feeling is going to help you successfully complete this 21 day program. If there comes a point when you are wondering why you are doing this program, tap into that feeling as an empathy reference point for yourself. Feeling the power of ecstatic engagement reminds you of the reward for doing the work.

Celebrate Today

"Tell me, what is it you plan to do with your one
wild and precious life?"

~ Mary Oliver

Celebrate your uniqueness right now. There is no other person in the world like you. Despite daily life, each of us can find a reason to celebrate because there is no one else who has our smile, our tears, our bills (darn it!)—and the list goes on. The ideal cause for celebration!

Begin your morning fresh, bright and in gratitude for the sun rising. Crawling back under the covers causes you to lose time and sets the stage for a crisis habit. Resistance simply means you will have to deal with it longer. If this applies to you, decide right now to make a change. Decide to start your day as though an incredible mystery is unfolding to rejuvenate your life.

Upon awakening, before you get out of bed, stretch each limb fully (think cat). Once out of bed, reach for the ceiling while standing on your tiptoes. Continue to stretch your shoulders forward and back, bending from the waist from side to side. As you are stretching, visualize your ideal day. The physical and mental stretching jumpstarts your circulation and opens your mind for a wonderful day. Now you are ready for an incredible day.

So wear your party pants, spend a little more time on your hair, and listen to some really great music on your travels. Every time you connect with someone—anyone—have a smile ready and a kind word. Each friendly connection will give you the gift of happiness and joy. This is all about you and your celebration.

Exercises

Look at least five new people in the eye with a smile on your face and acknowledge how fabulous today is. (If they want to know why, let them know you found the key to life!)

Consider what a perfect celebration looks like for you—and plan it! Your mind doesn't know if it's real or a memory, so it will work to create those circumstances to make it true. Feel free to invite the mariachi band!

Stand in front of a mirror and look deeply into the eyes of the amazing person looking back at you. Say "I love how you unique you are, and I am going to love you better today than yesterday." Repeat at least three times. (And if you find yourself still looking in the mirror an hour later, know that you've filled your personal love quota and it's ok to get on with your day…)

Before going to sleep tonight, reflect on your day. Write your feelings and thoughts about the day and how your new attitude affected the events of the day.

Reflections

Celebrate the happiness that friends are always giving, make every day a holiday and celebrate just living!

~ Amanda Bradley

Reflections

"Nothing great has ever been achieved except by those who dared believe something inside them was superior to circumstances."

~ *Bruce Barton*

Day 2

Count Your Blessings

"We tend to forget that happiness doesn't come as a result of getting something we don't have, but rather of recognizing and appreciating what we do have."

~ Frederick Keonig

What is a blessing anyway? It is a gift that has been given to you just because of who you are—it can be anything in the eye of the beholder, as they say. It could be that you are grateful for the sun rising, for knowing the date, or for looking forward to a date. Today, hopefully, you find they are too numerous to count.

Blessings don't care where you live, your financial situation, or your relationship with your family, or even your job. Blessings are all about what you appreciate about your life. Were you able to get out of bed unassisted, bathe, dress and eat? Count that as a blessing! Start with the small stuff and work your way up.

Today, as you are driving in your car, walking down the street, or just standing on the sidewalk, or maybe you are in a wheelchair, look up. What do you see? Do you see a gray, blue, cloud puffs or a mix of all? Perhaps it is raining or snowing. How often do you take the time to look up? Looking up is a reminder that you are a part of something larger, that you CAN renew and rejuvenate your life. In fact, that's your job. You are in charge! This, by the way, is a blessing.

Exercises

Define what a "blessing" is for yourself. What does a blessing look and feeling like?

Now think about how many you've been able to give to someone else lately.

Make a concerted effort to give blessings to at least five new people today. How did that make you feel?

How many blessings do you receive in just one day? Today, for example? Carry a blessings book (some might call it a little pocket-sized spiral notebook) for the day and make note of how often
you feel blessed.

As you give, you shall receive. Give something (or your time) to a charity organization of your choice today.

Before retiring tonight, reflect on your day. Write your feelings and thoughts about the day and how your new attitude affected the events of the day.

Reflections

"Blessed is he who has learned to admire but not envy, to follow but not imitate, to praise but not flatter, and to lead but not manipulate."

~ *William A. Ward*

Reflections

"Develop an "attitude of gratitude." Say thank you to everyone you meet for everything they do for you."

~ Brian Tracy

Write Your Goals

"You are successful the moment you start moving toward a worthwhile goal."

~ Chuck Carlson

"I have measured out my life in coffee spoons," wrote T. S. Eliot in *The Love Song of J. Alfred Prufrock*. Have you ever really looked at the measure of a coffee spoon? If one must measure life, why use such a small measure? Why not use a full measuring cup, a pint jar, a quart jar, a gallon jug, a peck or a bushel? Why settle for a coffee spoon? There are so many other ways to measure life -why not an inch, a foot, a yard or a mile? Why measure when one can live life in such a way that one would need a limitless measure? Make life so enjoyable that the biggest measure falls short. Get back on purpose and achieve your best life!

If you could do and be anything you wanted, what would it be and what would you do? Remember that age has nothing to do with your goals—the only real deadline is when you are six feet under. And, since you are committed to this program, you haven't reached the state of being and doing what you want yet... which means, there is no time like the present to start!

You know what's ideal, so now it's time to distill that into SMART goals; that is, specific, measurable, achievable, realistic and timely goals. Vague goals get vague results. The SMART-er your goals are, the more likely you are to make them happen.

Exercises

Create three new goals that relate to living your best life. It is important that these three goals are achievable in the next two weeks—we are all about making change happen quickly!

Complete the following phrase: "I know I am successful by_____." These statements then become the guides for SMART goals.

Write a letter to yourself imagining what your life will look like from the vantage point of a future date and looking back on today. Will you note that it was the day you started your rejuvenation process OR will you say it was the day you could have started? Will you say "WOW, I made it happen starting that day" OR "I started but it took too much effort?" If it seems like it is taking to much effort, it could be that you are not aiming for the right goal. Remember, no one sees the letter; it is for your eyes only, unless you choose to share. And if you make that choice, remember that you are diluting your power to manifest and that this is about you anyway–so share carefully!

Remember to journal your observations about the day. Pay attention to what thoughts or fears came up around your goals—these are your habit elimination plan.

Reflections

"You may not accomplish every goal you set—no one does—but what really matters is having goals and going after them wholeheartedly."

~ Les Brown

Reflections

"I find it fascinating that most people plan their vacation with better care than they do their lives. Perhaps that is because escape is easier than change."

~ Jim Rohn

Day 4

Eliminate Woulda, Shoulda, Coulda

"At this moment, the room you are in is full of radio waves. You know they are there, even though you can't see them. You know that if you turned on a radio and tuned in to a particular station, you could hear them. You just have to tune in to the right frequency. To get the music you want in your life, your highest success, you just have to tune in to right station and lock on."

~ James Ray,
The Science of Success

How often have you heard or said "woulda, shoulda or coulda" and realized that it was wasted effort and energy? These are dead words. They mean nothing. Nothing can be accomplished using those words. Nothing equals zero! Using those words ensures that you continue to live your life in crisis.

These words do not accomplish anything in the present. In fact, these little words have big meaning in that there is something in the past that was not done and you are living with the regret.

Living with regret is living in the past and not allowing you the opportunities for accepting the challenges of today. Each time you lament "woulda, shoulda, coulda," you allow the present to slip into oblivion. You are losing the opportunities to enjoy life right now and continue to give yourself lament over what "woulda, coulda shoulda" been. Life is a gift to be lived in the present with an eye to the future. This is not to suggest that we ignore the past, but use the past as a learning guide for decisions made today. Use the past as if it were a rudder, not a compass.

Exercises

Consider what regrets are holding you back from living your best life right now. Take each one, roll it around in your mind, and test it to see if it's real. Is there anything you can do to change it? If not, reframe it in your mind as a gift—a learning opportunity that got you here today and which will help you make different decisions in the future. Note the greater lesson in each situation in order to honor it for your future.

Honor the discoveries of each of your regrets by turning them into a positive affirmation. For example, your regret about skipping school in your youth is now "I appreciate and value education, and will be present at every opportunity." You may want to post these in your environment so you can visually reinforce your new knowingness.

Eliminate these words from your thought patterns. Place a rubber band around your wrist for the day. Each time you find yourself thinking or saying, "woulda, shoulda, coulda", snap the rubber band and say "cancel, cancel", then replace that thought with a positive affirmation. "This is where I am supposed to be in my life at this time". This ensures that you are living consciously your best life in the moment.

Before going to sleep tonight, reflect on your day. Did the rubber band help to keep you on track? Do you understand the lessons from your past in a new way? Write your feelings and thoughts about the day and how your new attitude affected the events of the day.

Reflections

"When the impossibility has been eliminated, whatever remains, no matter how improbable…is possible."

~ Sir Arthur ConanDoyle

Reflections

"Failures are divided into two classes—those who thought and never did, and those who did and never thought."

~ John Charles Salak

Day 5

Live With Integrity

"No more duty can be urged upon those who are entering the great theatre of life than simple loyalty to their best convictions."

~ Edwin H. Chapin

Integrity is a quality that keeps you morally and ethically sound. Once you live with integrity, dishonesty (in any form) will simply not be in your life. You are the most important person with whom to practice integrity. Make a pact that you will honor your word to yourself and others. Be known by the fact that you honor your word.

This will be more difficult for some people because of previous habitual behaviors and continued attitudes. Practicing integrity requires change, which is uncomfortable. (If it were easy, would you be in this program?)

Change itself requires viewing life in a different way—stepping out of the box. Change causes tension, as the new desired system bumps up against or attempts to eliminate the old system. We humans generally don't see our own boxes, which makes it difficult to see how to step outside of it. The box represents your everyday life—the things you do, the people you associate with, the activities where you spend your time. Having "butterflies in your stomach" is actually a physical feeling to gauge that you are on the right track in making change.

Living consistently with integrity may seem a small change, but the result is potentially huge. It takes courage to be this honest with yourself. If something is not right for you, hurts someone else, or is inauthentic, it is the exact place to start practicing integrity. And as you get rid of non-integrity, it will get easier over time (because you are already in integrity!).

Exercises

Ask three people whom you respect the following questions—"how do you see me?" and "what do I need to know?" Encourage them to be open and honest because this is information to help guide your personal change process. When they share their thoughts with you, remain objective and distill the significant information into what is meaningful for you. If you have a "ping" reaction, it is definitely something for you to look at and determine what changes you need to make to live in integrity.

Consider any relationships that are no longer in your life. Was a lack of integrity a factor in losing that relationship? Could you have handled anything better in that relationship? If yes, turn that into a learning opportunity for current and future relationships.

If you find yourself telling little white lies, or bending the truth, for ANY reason, look at the real reason without blaming the other person. Is it about them—or you?

Have you done everything you said you would with your day? Broken promises to yourself are the most damaging because they set up self-sabotage patterns. And how can you keep your integrity with others when you aren't able to keep it with the most important person –yourself? While reflecting tonight, review the information you received from these exercises. Journal how being congruent with integrity could and/or has already impacted your life, and what changes you are making for living your best life with integrity.

Reflections

"Be daring, be different, be impractical, be anything that will assert integrity of purpose and imaginative vision against the play-it-safers, the creatures of the commonplace, the slaves of the ordinary."

~ Sir Cecil Beaton

Reflections

"Trust yourself. Create the kind of self that you will be happy to live with all your life. Make the most of yourself by fanning the tiny, inner sparks of possibility into flames of achievement."

~ Foster C. McClellan

Day 6

Add Value

"Truly great dancers are those who make their partners look good. Like Fred Astaire."

~ Melanie Svoboda

You've probably seen advertisements that "throw" in something as a "value-added" product as an incentive to sweeten the deal. Just like trying to sell a product, we are selling ourselves to our world every day. Many people choose to do only what is required or, sometimes, even less. In making that choice, what people don't realize is that they are only turning their own light down by not showing up and being all of who they are —the person hurt most by holding back is themselves.

Add value to everything you do today. How can you add value to your life? It is simple things... going the extra mile, doing the little bit extra, arriving a few minutes early or staying a little later to do more than is required Add five minutes to your exercise routine or do two more repetitions, drink more water, write one more letter, handle one more email, make one more phone call, just one more... After all, it only makes your day that much better for you.

Exercises

Add personal value today by finding one positive thing to say to each person you meet today, even if you are annoyed with that person. Ask if there is something that you are doing to contribute to that sense of annoyance and if there is something that you can do to add value to their day. You may find that your perception changes about the situation when you take responsibility for adding value.

Think of ways you can add value at your job and in your family. How many of you have young children? And when you arrive home, they demand some of your attention. How often do you say, "not now, I'm tired"? What do you think the difference would be if you took just five minutes to address the child's needs? Most of the time, children only have a few minutes to be bothered with adults because they have to go play. So add value to your children's lives by spending a few extra minutes with them.

Go out of your way to do a little extra for yourself. Adding value to your own life ensures that you are living your best life every day. Buy flowers for yourself, take a few extra minutes with your coffee, take a walk at lunchtime...create self-appreciation rituals that remind you how valuable you are to yourself.

At day's end, reflect on your day and write your thoughts. Remember that writing calls into being whatever you desire. Adding value to your life and to the lives of those around you is an important part of living your best life.

Reflections

"One's life has value so long as one attributes value to the life of others, by means of love, friendship, indignation, and compassion."

~ *Simone DeBeauvoir*

Reflections

"What you have to do and the way you have to do it is incredibly simple. Whether you are willing to do it, that's another matter."

~ Peter F. Drucker

Think "Right" Thoughts

"Until thought is linked with purpose there is no intelligent accomplishment."

~ As a Man Thinketh

Every action begins with a thought. Monitor your thoughts very carefully; what you think is what you create. Your thoughts manifest in your life in everything you do. Thoughts lead to feelings which lead to action which leads to results. If you don't like the results you are getting, understand the thoughts you have been thinking that created them.

For example, if one of your goals is to lose weight but all you think about is food, your next meal, or how you don't want to be fat, you will likely continue to stay hungry and overweight. However, if you change your thought patterns about your weight by replacing them with "I am my ideal weight, I exercise and take care of my body, and I make healthy food choices," you will likely start to experience progress.

Instead of saying what you don't want, say what you do want. You will find that your thoughts will make all the difference. When you find the OLD thoughts sliding

34

in, say "cancel, cancel" in your mind and replace it with your new desired way of thinking so that you can manifest that new you. Old thought patterns (habits) are comfortable and familiar, so they will linger as long as you let them. If it becomes necessary, shout them out!

Exercises

Throughout conversations today, notice the language that is in your mind before you speak. Is it positive, authentic, sincere? Or is it judgmental, harsh and negative? Is it your voice or someone else's that you accept as your own? Do you have to "spin" the words that come out of your mouth from your thoughts? If you find that you are changing the verbal words you say in order to be acceptable, chances are your thoughts are sabotaging how you show up in the world. Once you notice that your thoughts are not supporting your conversations, you can proactively change your thoughts—and then notice how your communications and relationships shift!

Observe your thoughts as you consider your day. What language do you use in your own mind? If you find that your thoughts are different from how you would talk to a friend, your thoughts are probably not supporting you in living your best life. How would you feel if you were being yelled at while you were trying to create a piece of art? Because that is what is happening if your thoughts are too hard on you. Being your best starts in your own mind first—shift your thoughts to be helpful to you, using the language you would in talking to a close friend.

Watch how others communicate; if you see body language that doesn't match the words, chances are their thoughts are not matching their words either. This is not to judge or criticize others; rather, this is to see that they are human, just as you are, and that everyone could be their best a lot easier if they monitored their thoughts.

It's likely that your thoughts are showing up in your body language too. Be aware of how your thoughts are contributing to your body language.

Ask a close friend to listen to you as you talk about your day. Ask that friend to monitor how many times you are negative or somehow undermining your day's events through language. We become so ingrained with negative thinking that it is challenging to see/hear it for ourselves. Remember that this is not setting yourself up to be hurt; this is an exercise in self-development. Your friend will be your mirror to show you the power of your thoughts throughout your day and in your language. Honor that by changing your thoughts to be more supportive of the most important person in your world—you.

Imagine that you are in a laboratory, and scientists were able to tune in to your thoughts. How would you feel about that? If you could only think one thought, and they monitored you, what would it be? And now, imagine that you are out of that laboratory. What did you learn about your thinking patterns? If you could change only one thought, what would it be? (and now, the next one... and the next one...) Before going to sleep tonight, reflect on your day. Write your feelings and thoughts about the day and how your new thinking affected the events of the day.

End of the First Week

"You are unique, and if that is not fulfilled, then something has been lost."

~ Martha Graham

Isn't this exciting! You are 1/3 of the way on your journey to rejuvenation, recapturing the spring in your step and being your best. Acknowledge yourself for the work you have done and accept yourself for where you are right now.

Check in with your thoughts; determine if there is any anger, defensiveness, or upset. Perhaps you are feeling calm, peaceful and that all is right with the world. Any or all of your feelings are natural, expected, and okay. Remember, you are in a rejuvenation process and sometimes things will feel uncomfortable—and they should! That tells you that you are doing things differently.

Concentrate on your new best life you are making for yourself. Remind yourself of the feeling of ecstatic engagement to feel the joy that is yours—let it pull you forward into positive action. And continue the journey you have begun to live your best life—NOW!

Reflections

*"The Law of Attraction attracts to you everything
you need, according to the nature of your life. Your
environment and financial condition are the perfect
reflection of your habitual thinking.
Thought rules the world."*

~ Joseph Edward Murphy

Reflections

"Your own mind is a sacred enclosure into which nothing harmful can enter except by your promotion."

~ Ralph Waldo Emerson

Day 8

Stop Procrastinating

"The difference between great people and everyone else is that great people create their lives actively, while everyone else is created by their lives, passively waiting to see where life takes them next. The difference between the two is the difference between living fully and just existing."

~ Michael E. Gerber

There are two days in the week that means nothing to us but are used frequently—yesterday and tomorrow. If anything offers a "free gift tomorrow", knowing that tomorrow never really is here today, do you think anyone ever gets that free gift? It's like Wimpy offering to gladly pay on Tuesday for getting his hamburger today. Tomorrow is a future state—it's not here right now, today. Yesterday is gone, tomorrow isn't here yet and the present is our gift right now.

"I'll start writing my paper tomorrow", "I "shoulda" started it yesterday", "I "coulda" finished my laundry yesterday but I'll get to it tomorrow".... Most of the time, "woulda, shoulda and coulda" will come into use when we procrastinate. Today is the only day we have -so we owe it to ourselves to use it. Too often, we unfortunately find ourselves doing things at the last minute because we did not utilize the time we had today. Procrastinating is one of the easiest things to do in the world because it requires no effort, but it's one of the hardest habits to break—if we stop procrastinating, we might actually have to do something.

Think of it like this: Imagine that it's midnight, and you have a craving for really good ice cream. There's a 24-hour grocery store down the street, but you don't really want to make an ice cream run. But you really want the ice cream. You could wait until the light of day tomorrow but it just wouldn't be the same. So, if you really want that ice cream, you are going to the store right then. If you want something bad enough, there is no such thing as procrastination. Procrastination is a myth that people use to put off doing what needs to be done if they don't want to do it. The solution to procrastination is discipline.

Exercises

When was the last time you handled something you'd been putting off? And how did you feel when you got it done? Remember that and anchor that sense of accomplishment in your mind and body—write the words that describe that sensation so you can see them until you finish all your delayed projects.

Observe the signs of procrastination in your life— what is cluttered, overgrown, dusty, undone, in disrepair? Consider how your life is different (as in, where is it stuck) because of it AND how your life would be different if you handled that pile, cleaned that space, repaired that gizmo... Just noticing how your life has stalled as a result of not handling it could be enough motivation to get you moving.

Identify the top three projects that you have been putting off. Whatever they are, resolve today to begin to work on those projects. Clean out the clutter, finish your taxes, rearrange the closet, take the things to Goodwill that you have not used in two to three years—and feel good that you are helping someone who needs it. Why clutter your life with unused or outgrown stuff that depresses you and holds you back every time you see it? Go for your ice cream—resolve that today is the day you stop procrastinating.

Once you have confronted and released what used to be your procrastination habit, be sure to keep up the attention to detail as it happens and celebrate your ability to do so! On a weekly basis, take note of how you handling your life in the moment. Over time, you'll see that you have less back-ups or blockages—everything should be moving at life speed. With nothing building up waiting to get handled, you are living your best life!

Before going to sleep tonight, reflect on your day. Appreciate the new feeling of spaciousness and the confidence in knowing that the possessions you released will help someone else, that you are on top of your game, that your life doesn't have any more loose ends. Write your feelings and thoughts about the day and how your new attitude affected the events of the day.

Reflections

"Know the true value of time; snatch, seize, and enjoy every moment of it. No idleness, no delay, no procrastination; never put off till tomorrow what you can do today."

~ Lord Chesterfield

Reflections

"To be always intending to make a new and better life but never to find time to set about it is as to put off eating and drinking and sleeping from one day to the next until you're dead."

~ Og Mandino

Day 9

Perseverance

"... the backbone of success is usually found in old-fashioned, basic concepts like hard work, determination, good planning and perseverance."

~ Mia Hamm

Stick to the task. Complete what you start. How many times have you started a task and became distracted or interrupted? Somehow you never got back to the task. Sometimes a task will require more emotion, time and/or energy than you thought. Is your default mode to just give up or do you keep pushing on?

Sometimes the reward is just around the bend in the proverbial road, and if you quit, you won't find it. To reference another metaphor, if you can't see the light at the end of the tunnel, does that mean that the light isn't there or does it mean that you will see it with a little more effort?

Sticking to the task gives you the opportunity to live your best life—a life of expectation and excitement. If you stop before the mystery unfolds or the road bends, you will never know the excitement and joy of completion. Whenever you feel bewildered and want to quit, reflect back on—and celebrate—how far you have come. Remember life is a journey and this task is only one small part. Once the task is completed, celebrate and look forward to the next opportunity to create your best life.

Exercises

In looking back on your life, what projects have you given up on too soon? Is there a pattern? If it were to happen again, how would you know whether to persevere? Take note of the signs of perseverance from the past to learn how to persevere for your future.

List up to three top priority projects that need your attention right now. Decide what you need to do to support yourself in persevering with them—and make it happen! It's easier than you may think.

If a project feels like it is taking too much effort and it's too difficult to persevere, consider what else might be happening with the project. Could it be that it is a project or commitment that is not reflecting your best life? If it is not the right place to put your time or energy, minimize or stop putting your energy into it and move on to something that is worth your investment.

Before going to sleep tonight, reflect on your day. What task did you find difficult? Was it difficult because you did not want to do it or because it took more time than you thought or because you didn't think it was that important? Write your feelings and thoughts about the day and how your new attitude affected the events of the day.

Reflections

"Patience and perseverance have a magical effect before which difficulties disappear and obstacles vanish."

~ John Quincy Adams

Reflections

"Most of the important things in the world have been accomplished by people who have kept on trying when there seemed to be no help at all."

~ Dale Carnegie

Day 10

Effort

"I've always believed that if you put in the work, the results will come. I don't do things half-heartedly. Because I know if I do, then I can expect half-hearted results."

~ Michael Jordan

How much do you want to live your best life? What are you willing to do to rejuvenate your life? And how much effort are you willing to put in to rejuvenate your life on purpose?

Putting time, attention, energy and resources into creating your best life is the only way you will create it for yourself. The effort is only because this requires a new way of thinking, believing that you can have—and deserve—what you want.

As children, we hear the word "no" four times as much as we hear the word "yes" (and there are studies to this effect). Reprogramming yourself to forget about all of the "no, you can't" lessons you learned throughout life and replacing them with "yes I can" is deeply personal, powerful work. And it may take some effort.

When you embark on this journey, friends may ask what has come over you, why are you changing, and that they like you the way you were. All of which are completely natural—any system of which you are a part needs you to stay the same because if you change, you force IT to change. And it doesn't want to change—a natural state of being is to stay in "homeostasis", which is a condition of sameness. At the same time, growth happens gradually in nature—nothing is forced. You, desiring to be living your best life now, are pushing change to happen quickly. And you will experience the effects of that process through the world around you.

Exercises

Invite your friends to join you on your journey, share with them what you know about living your best life. Some of them will join you while others may think you are a little bit crazy. More importantly, don't let anyone dissuade you from continuing on your journey. Rather, resolve to be stronger than anyone who tries to put you down or hold you back. Remember this is the only life you have and you get to choose how you want to live it.

Read "The Little Engine That Could" and "The Places You Will Go." If you thought these were children's stories, think again. If you think you can, you can; if you think you can't, you're right. Whatever you think is true for you.

Consider the projects or life areas that seem to take the most effort. Is this because they really do take more work or is it because they really aren't important to you so they feel like more effort? If you see the rewards and want to keep going, remind yourself that the pay-off is proportionate to the effort exerted. And if not, let them go so you can put your effort into something meaningful and significant for you and your best life.

Take note of the feelings that come up for you as you rejuvenate your life. Rejuvenation is a release of whatever doesn't support you, and that can bring up all kinds of emotion. Releasing people, relationships, patterns, habits, old programs, clutter, etc. is bound to bring up your issues and emotions related to them. Honor the original purpose of that person, relationship, habit, etc. and move forward in taking care of you now in the interest of living your best life and knowing that you are honoring your true, authentic self. It's hard to give up the familiar, but it's also necessary to call in your new being. Be in gratitude, ask for a smooth release, and be open to feeling your feelings in order to let them go. Set your intention for new, supportive people, relationships, habits, etc.

Before going to sleep tonight, reflect on your day. Did you find yourself concentrating more on what rejuvenation means for you? Did you get to reevaluate what is really important? Give yourself permission to change your mind if after you reevaluated you decided that you want something different. Just resolve to continue the program with a new outlook. Tune in to your feelings and thoughts about the day and journal about the affects of your new attitude on the events of the day.

Reflections

"If you have a positive attitude and constantly strive to give your best effort, eventually you will overcome your immediate problems and find you are ready for greater challenges."

~ Pat Riley

Reflections

"Satisfaction lies in the effort, not in the attainment, full effort is full victory."

~Mahatma Gandhi

Responsibility

"Always do right. It will gratify some people and astonish the rest."

~ Mark Twain

For whom are you responsible? If you answered yourself, you are on the right track. So many times, it is easy to get caught-up in taking responsibility for others (family, friends and others) without room for thought in taking responsibility for self. This is not to say that you should not take care of family and friends, but that you must take care of yourself first in order to be capable of helping everyone else. Think airplane safety; you must put on your oxygen mask first, and then help your neighbor or child.

You are responsible for doing what is appropriate for you. Determine what is appropriate for you, how life feels for you, what you want to reflect in your life, and how you live your life. Being full self-responsible opens unlimited possibility and allows you to express who you are consistently and from a position of strength. Upon taking full responsibility for your life, you will discover contentment, for it is on your decisions, choices and personal accountability that your best life exists.

Exercises

Take an inventory of the people around you; for how many of them are you responsible? And is it truly your responsibility to care for them? In some traditions, it is believed to be an act of sabotage, not of love, to do too much in caring for someone. You are robbing them of their ability to learn their life lessons. If you find that you are too responsible for others, it is time to let go.

Define what "responsibility" means for you. It is possible to change only what we know already; we cannot change what is not understood. If you feel a deep, abiding sense of responsibility for others, it may be a pull to give to others in a professional, or channeled, way. If you find that you are putting others first, it may be time to look at the way these distractions are affecting your ability to take care of yourself. It is always easier to focus outside rather than do the necessary work inside ourselves. Have you ever heard of "backseat driver"? Worse, are you one?

As you move through your day, note what you do out of habit or routine that is not yours to care for; the intention is not for you to become an island. The idea is that you notice where you are putting your time and energy outside of yourself, and decide consciously if that is a wise and appropriate investment.

Before going to sleep tonight, reflect on your day. Write your feelings and thoughts about the day and how your new attitude affected the events of the day.

Reflections

You cannot escape the responsibility of tomorrow by evading it today."

~ Abraham Lincoln

Reflections

"Every right implies a responsibility; every opportunity, an obligation, every possession, a duty."

~ John D. Rockefeller

Day 12

Initiative

"The difference between getting somewhere and nowhere is the courage to make an early start. The fellow that sits still and does just what he is told will never be told to do big things."

~ Charles M. Schwab

Do you move into action or do you wait for others to move you into action? Do you design your life based on decisions others made for you? Do you live your life based on what you think others want from you?

Imagine what would happen if you take the initiative in designing your best life. Designing your life relieves you of the stress of always having to be right and live up to others' expectations. And designing your life can be easier than you think with a little attention and initiative.

Taking the initiative to rejuvenate your life on purpose gives you the opportunity to live your best life by giving you the freedom to discover who you are and the greater truth of why you are here. Armed with the knowledge of knowing that you are perfect, you can achieve your best life based on what you want. Move into action today. Design the life you want.

Exercises

Visualize an ideal day in your best life. Play it in your mind like a movie – where are you? What are you wearing? What are you doing? Is anyone else with you? How do you feel? As you watch the movie of your best life, notice any physical or emotional sensations you may have—notice how you are breathing. Once you have seen your "day in the best life" movie, share it with a friend. Ask them to help you clarify this movie; that is, they will summarize what they think you are saying and play it back to you verbally. This engages all of your senses in creating your best life.

Identify three projects in your life right now where you could be, and want to be, showing initiative. Remember, this is not about the urgent stuff that is screaming at you, but the important things that you really want to do. Translation: for example, this is not about paying the bills but about taking French lessons. Pick one and take initiative right now!

Consider if there are any projects that are in stagnation mode right now; are they really necessary to complete or is it ok to simply release them? If you need to not do any more with them, let them go. And if it's time to pump up the energy, determine the best way to take initiative in the next 24 hours. And then do it!

Before going to sleep tonight, reflect on your day. On what did you take initiative today? Did taking initiative lead you to rejuvenation—do you feel different as a result? Or are you going back to the "comfort" of old habits? If you feel disappointed with yourself that you "waited" so long to rejuvenate your life, notice the feeling and let it go—it's not supporting you in moving forward in your best life. In acknowledging the feelings, create three columns on a piece of paper; on the left side write what you are feeling, in the middle write why you feel this way and on the right side write actions you will take to continue to live your best life.

Reflections

*"Initiative is doing the right thing
without being told."*

~ Victor Hugo

Reflections

"The four cornerstones of character on which the structure of this nation was built are: initiative, imagination, individuality, and independence."

~ Eddie Rickenbacker

Day 13

Motivation

"What you can do, or dream you can, begin it.
Boldness has genius, power, and magic in it."

~ Goethe

Okay, now you really get to make some choices. You've worked through a lot of information and processed how to get action in achieving your best life right now. This is all about the level of motivation you have to do something different based on what you've learned. Motivation comes from within—only you can motivate you. Motivation means wanting something bad enough to do something to get it. And you must be motivated, because you are still in the program. Ask yourself again the following questions.

> Do you want to change your life?
> Do you want to live your best life?
> Are you willing to put in the effort to rejuvenate your life?
> Are you content with living in crisis and/or chaos?

You get to choose. And if you choose not to choose, it is still a choice. If you don't do anything different today, then your life tomorrow will look exactly like it does right now—how do you feel about that?

Your determination is what powers your change to living your best life. Determine that you want to have the life of your dreams—your best life - and you want it enough to do what it takes to make the change.

Sustaining motivation can be inconsistent—it can take effort, especially with a major transformation. When motivation lags, remind yourself of the goal(s), of when you felt the energy of ecstatic engagement, and get back on track. Granted, you may have setbacks in sustaining motivation, but having determination and a passionate goal to pull you forward eases you through those tough times.

How do you know you are living your best life? What does that feel and look like for you? Only you will know for yourself, because it is different for everyone. For some, it may be a sense of freedom, a joyous feeling from within and that life on the outside is a reflection of the freshness you feel on the inside. For others, it may be that they are deciding what their day looks like each and every day. It's important that you know what you best life looks like because that will motivate you to stay on track with creating it.

Exercises

On a scale of 1–1,000, what would you say your level of motivation is for living your best life? If it is less than 1,000, why? If you are not motivated, you are not going to make changes (especially during tough times). Find a picture that represents your goal and place it in a visible spot in your space—allow it to pull you forward on a daily basis.

Go rent "Million Dollar Baby." This movie is guaranteed to show you motivation in action.

Look at the times in your life when you haven't achieved exactly what you wanted. Now consider your motivation level around that goal. What is the relationship? If you find that your motivation wasn't really there, think about how it could have been different with the right motivation. If that's how you feel now about ANYTHING in your life, it is time to revisit the motivation factor.

As you move through your day, notice what motivates you. Is it habit, pattern or true desire? Is your motivation coming from taking positive action toward a goal or moving away from the pain of not achieving it? For example, some people want to look a certain way and take care of themselves accordingly; the converse is also true. Other people do not want to look a certain way, and that motivates them to take care of themselves accordingly. From a basic biological perspective, we are programmed to move toward pleasure and away from pain—which is the way your motivation works.

Notice how people around you are motivated—what are their main motivators? Can you relate with any of them? What do you think are the most common motivators for our culture?

At day's end, take time to reflect on your day. Write your feelings and thoughts about the day and how your new awareness about motivation affected the events of the day.

Reflections

"Be miserable. Or motivate yourself. Whatever has to be done, it's always your choice."

~ Wayne Dyer

Reflections

"People often say that motivation doesn't last. Well, neither does bathing— that's why we recommend it daily."

~ Zig Ziglar

Day 14

Focus

"The ability to simplify means to eliminate the
unnecessary so that the necessary may speak."

~ Hans Hofmann

Focus is what makes a light beam become a laser beam, capable of cutting through steel. Without focus, light remains scattered and harmless. Focus renders what would seem to be an impossible task (cutting steel with a beam of light) and makes it nearly an everyday occurrence.

The same is true for you in rejuvenating your life on purpose. Making conscious choices about changing in order to live your best life requires focus. Focus allows what is no longer necessary, supportive or unhealthy to fall away, and allows us to clearly see what is significant, healthy and needed in moving forward.

Exercises

Consider where you have been lacking focus. Do you have projects that feel out of control? Do you feel scattered in your day? Are you foggy in knowing your priorities? Wherever you see that you are lacking focus, create an action plan to focus on immediate next steps. Follow your focus to channel your efforts in a consolidated way to get results.

Look at the sources of static, or white noise, that prevents your focus. Consider such things as: environment, relationships, scheduling system, job, social obligations, drama from sources outside you, etc. If you can "see" the static, or the patterns that lead to static for you, go to the source. Determine if you are responsible for the static; if you are, it is time to address it. And if this is not your issue, just say no to static!

Reconsider your goals in this program; be sure they still reflect your best life. Take note of what you have achieved so far. If your progress isn't what you had hoped for, it could be an indicator of static that has pulled you off course or distracted you. Simply eliminate the static, reevaluate your goals (and your motivation), and get moving in a deliberately focused way.

Take time to assimilate your thoughts from the day about focus. Note if there is a pattern or habit that you need to address that will allow you to focus more clearly in the future. Make an effort to notice your focus, and create an action plan to support your newfound focus. Journaling your discoveries will help you to focus your thoughts.

Reflections

"Don't dwell on what went wrong. Instead, focus on what to do next. Spend your energies on moving forward toward finding the answer."

~ Denis Waitley

Reflections

"The key to success is to focus our conscious mind on things we desire, not things we fear."

~ Brian Tracy

End of the Second Week

"What we believe and how we believe determine our reality…. when you change your beliefs, your experiences will change."

~ Harry Palmer

Celebrate; today is the fourteenth day that you have enjoyed the program! You are two-thirds of the way through to living your best life. This process may have brought up some unexpected feelings (doubt, trepidation, confusion)—congratulations! Those are exactly the feelings that you need to process as learning opportunities to release them, rejuvenate yourself, and create your new life on purpose.

Or you may be feeling pretty good about yourself and enjoying the rejuvenation process—give yourself a hug and standing ovation! Remember, you desire a different future, and you are doing something different to make that happen. Embracing the change is a good way to keep going!

Reflect on your goal(s) and how far you have come in the last two weeks. How many curves in the road have you navigated successfully? How many times have you seen the light at the end of the tunnel and known that it was a mirror reflecting your radiance? How many compliments have you received from others? What is the feeling you are experiencing today? Are you feeling joy that you have stayed on track, with excitement and anticipation at what is around the bend? Your emotions are messages that let you know you are experiencing a transformation process. Your intellect will work with your emotions in that you are doing all of this on purpose.

In continuing this rejuvenation on purpose, know that you may feel grief as the old way of being dies. That is perfectly natural. We have to have endings in order to have beginnings—ask what you need to release in order to continue your journey. Rather than staying stuck in what was, let go of the old in order to welcome in what can be. Keep your eye on your goal, knowing the power it has to keep you moving forward toward creating your best life.

It is important that you stick with your rejuvenation process. Stay focused, stay motivated, and stay in action! Concentrate on living your best life. If you find that you are wavering, you are the one who will be hurt by not living the best life you deserve. Don't let that happen—you've come too far. Breathe, vision living your best life right now, and set your intention to reinvigorate your commitment. You are DOING this with everything you've got because your best life is riding on it! Keep up the momentum!

Day 15

Confidence

"The first secret of success? Self-trust."

~ Ralph Waldo Emerson

Confidence is not a false bravado kind of feeling but a feeling of sureness about what you are doing and being. Center your mind and actions in the present, using your past successes to guide you. Confidence comes from knowing that you are on track with being who you are regardless of external circumstances. Filling yourself up with the power of all that is you radiates self assurance on every level. And, in social situations, no one else knows what's in your head... the only way anyone can read your confidence level is by what you show them through action and by what they feel through your personal energy.

Knowing that you are in the process of successfully creating your best life on purpose, and taking action accordingly are the keys to having what you want in your life. You know that you can, and will, continue your powerful transformation to live your best life with confidence. You are embracing today with self assurance to move forward, knowing that whatever happens in your life, you will be able to handle it.

Trusting yourself to make the right decisions gives you the ability to enjoy living your best life. Part of making the right decisions is the ability to trust yourself to see all aspects of a situation or issue to choose most appropriately for yourself, and then create the environments to support the fulfillment of your needs. Acting from your inner sense of confidence allows you to live fully in the moment.

Exercises

Attend a social event and make yourself known to at least three new people. Project your confidence in conversation and note how it feels.

Identify a previous situation where you lacked confidence; feel that experience in your body. Now recall a situation where you exuded confidence; feel that experience in your body. What was the difference between these two feelings? How do you experience confidence in your body?

Interview someone you know about how confidence, or the lack of it, has affected their life. Learn by their experience how to handle your confidence effectively.

Think of someone you respect and look up to for guidance. What does this person do or how do they act that lets you know about their confidence levels? What can you learn from them about projecting your own confidence? And what would you do to let a protege know that you feel confident in your best life?

As you move through your day, notice if / how your thoughts are affecting your confidence levels. It would be natural to see a correlation between positive thoughts and positive confidence levels. Create a mental mantra about increasing or maintaining your confidence.

Reflect on how confidence has affected your life up until now. Write your feelings and thoughts about how your new understanding of confidence will affect living your best life.

Reflections

"If you have no confidence in self, you are twice defeated in the race of life. With confidence, you have won even before you have started."

~ *Marcus Garvey*

Reflections

"I am optimistic and confident in all that I do. I affirm only the best for myself and others. I am the creator of my life and my world. I meet daily challenges gracefully and with complete confidence. I fill my mind with positive, nurturing, and healing thoughts."

~ *Alice Potter*

Day 16

Caring

"What is as important as knowledge?" asked the mind. "Caring and seeing with the heart," answered the soul."

~ *Flavia*

We humans are a social lot; it's just the way we are programmed. Let others know that you care about them and their well-being. Show your appropriate concern for others every day through small gestures of respect. Ask questions to understand better how to care for them; it's important not to assume that you know what others need.

Caring for someone else is not about you or your ego... it's about connecting with them in the way they need or want. Make sure that you are not perceived as nosy or a busybody, and don't force help if it's not welcomed. Solicit from others the best way they would like you for you to show your concern.

A good way to gauge how to treat other people is to treat them the way you want to be treated. Do make them feel important, safe and cared for—as the valuable treasure that they are. And remember to take good care of yourself, too.

Exercises

Look around and see who (or what) needs some good care in your world. Take the time to find out what you can do to make a positive difference. Resolve to do at least one random act of kindness somewhere, somehow on a daily basis. (And then follow through!)

Volunteer at a local non-profit organization on a weekly basis. Choose a cause that has meaning for you, and know that you are helping to make the world a better place one person/hour at a time.

Define what "caring" means for you. Create a list of activities or gestures that you appreciate, and reference that list not only for you but for others as well.

Before going to sleep tonight, reflect on your day. Was there an opportunity in your day to show concern for someone or something? Did you accept the opportunity and show concern of did you let it slip by? Journal about how you made a difference for someone else by caring about them today.

Reflections

"Every one of us needs to show how much we care for each other and, in the process, care for ourselves."

~ *Diana, Princess of Wales*

Reflections

"A smile is the light in your window that tells others that there is a caring, sharing person inside."

~ Denis Waitley

Common Sense

"You cannot teach a man anything; you can only help him to find it within himself."

~ Galileo

Common sense is the sixth sense—that inner knowing of what is okay and not okay. Common sense discerns the appropriate and the inappropriate way to behave, thing to do, words to say and attitude to display. Common sense will be your guide to being congruent while you are rejuvenating your life and inventing new ways of being.

Use your common sense when making judgments about living your best life. When things go awry, it's time to pay close attention to your sixth sense.

Physically, this sixth sense is located in two places in your body. First, the small intestine has the same shape, is made of the same substance and secretes the same chemicals as the brain—this is what we think of as a "gut" feeling. Second, it is more commonly known that the sixth sense is located between your eyebrows. Some people call this the "third eye", and in Indian healing traditions, this is the sixth chakra. This is the feeling that always guides you to appropriate actions through inner knowingness.

Sometimes your sixth sense will tell you one thing while your rational intellect is telling you another. Learn to listen to your sixth sense; it is an inner guiding system that will never lead you astray.

Exercises

Have a comfortable seat and close your eyes. Ask for your common sense to help you answer a question. In answer, you may experience a sensation, get a picture or think a word; whatever it is, pay attention to the message and how it is communicated. This is the primary language of your common sense, and it is available for you to access to help you with any questions at any time.

As you move through your day, pay attention to how your common sense pops in. Remember it may be a quiet whisper or an inkling, and be fleeting in presence. Respect the "funny feeling" you get because it is a clue that there is something for you to know.

At day's end, reflect on your day. Were you in situations today where you listened to your sixth sense? Did issues arise today that caused you to ignore your sixth sense? What were the results of listening or ignoring? Write your feelings and thoughts about the day and how your sixth sense affected the events of the day.

Reflections

"Nothing astonishes people so much as common sense and plain dealing."

~ Ralph Waldo Emerson

Reflections

*"The three great essentials to achieve anything
worthwhile are: hard work, stick-to-itiveness and
common sense."*

~ Thomas A. Edison

Day 18

Resilience

"There is only one success—to be able to spend your life in your own way, and not to give others absurd maddening claims upon it".

~ Christopher Morley

Resilience is the ability to bounce back from a choice or situation that did not go the way you wanted or expected. Have you ever noticed that sometimes the people we perceive as having the most difficult things to overcome will excel in whatever they focus on? It seems that every time something knocks them down, they find a new way of coping and bounce back. In fact, resilience is proven to be one of the key factors in living a longer life, as well as enjoying an enhanced quality of life.

Resilience is an innate ability to recover from unexpected or negative situations. It is the ability to continue striving in the face of adversity - and to succeed. Rejuvenating your life requires resilience. Addressing where your life is out of alignment with integrity requires courage to confront and address those situations – it requires resilience to bounce back from such "learning opportunities". Fortunately, resilience is not limited in quantity and will support you as many times as you need in the process of creating your best life.

When you see the rocks in the road, will you navigate around them or run over them? Navigating around the rocks will give you different choices than running over them. Sometimes going around is easier and you don't lose your balance as quickly. In either case, listen to your common sense and make the decision that is best for you. And trust that your resilience will kick in if it's necessary.

Exercises

Watch a small child learn how to walk. Notice that no matter how many times it takes to get up from falling, the child gets up and adjusts to incorporate what they just learned. It is resilience in action.

Remember the biggest mistake you have ever made; then recall how you got beyond it. The gift of getting through such experiences is that you no longer fear making that mistake because you have survived and moved beyond it. Recall what you did and felt as you moved through it—these are the keys to your personal resilience.

Ask people you know what resilience means to them. Look for specific characteristics or patterns from what they describe to learn from their experiences; apply these to supporting your own process of resilience.

At the end of the day, reflect on your feelings and thoughts about resilience and how resilience has played a role in your life.

Reflections

"Man never made any material as resilient as the human spirit."

~ Bern Williams

Reflections

"It is inevitable that some defeat will enter even the most victorious life. The human spirit is never finished when it is defeated...it is finished when it surrenders."

~ Ben Stein

Day 19

Be Present

"They have no regret over the past, nor do they brood over the future. They live in the present; therefore they are radiant."

~ Buddha

Being present in the moment is a feeling of centeredness and focus on right now—not on what was nor on what will be. Being present releases any attachment to past or future, conscious of what is. Concentrate fully on whatever issue, task or behavior is at hand. Do not allow thoughts of "what you should, could or would" be doing to intrude. Put all of the outside thoughts that have nothing to do with the issue, task or behavior aside. This is especially important when being present with a significant other or family member.

In being present, you will discover a new "richness" in your conversations and relationships. You will no longer be answering their thoughts before they are finished, figuring out what to say ahead of time and not listening, or interrupting the flow of sharing. One-sided conversations will not exist in your world. Being present means listening to what the other person is saying without judging or formulating your reply. Too often you shortchange yourself because you are not allowing someone else to give fully and you are not able to give fully in return.

By being present, you are able to focus on what is happening as it happens. You will make conscious decisions based on information as it presents, in full knowledge and trust that you are drawing from all your available senses and inner wisdom.

Whatever you do today, be present. Be present in thought and action. When you begin to consistently practice being present, life will unfold in a beautiful and wondrous way. And you will assured of living your best life right now.

Exercises

Consider conversations you have had in the last 72 hours. For how many of them can you honestly say you were completely present with the other person? How could your ability to be completely attuned to that moment have affected the conversation / relationship? If you see a pattern in your communications, it is time to slow down and be present in your conversations.

In prioritizing your work day, do you find it necessary to multi-task at a high level all the time to get it all done? Would the quality of your performance improve if you were able to be present with one task or priority at a time? What can you do to shift into being present with your workload? Remember it will serve both you and your employer to be able to be more productive. Ask for help in managing your workload—that's why management exists in the workplace. And if you ARE the manager, your ability to be present with them and your workload sets an example for your employees.

Make a conscious effort to be present in every interaction today. Notice how it feels to really be with the subject of your presence. Feel it in your body. Be aware of how your presence affects your world. See patterns, behaviors, and routines that keep you from being present.

Take a moment to be present in reflecting on your day. Were you present today in all of your interactions? How did you feel? Write your observations, feelings and thoughts about how your ability to be present affects the world around you.

Reflections

"It is a mark of soulfulness to be present in the here and now. When we are present, we are not fabricating inner movies. We are seeing what is before us."

~John Bradshaw

Reflections

"A loser seldom lives in the present, but instead destroys the present by focusing on past memories or future expectations."

~Muriel James

Day 20

Get Involved

"The masters at the art of living make little distinction between their work and their play... They simply pursue their vision of excellence at whatever they do—leaving others to decide whether they are working or playing."

~ James Michener

No man (or woman!) is an island. It takes a village to raise a child. We are all one. Community is the natural by-product of people living in a geographical area. And part of our human programming is to contribute to something bigger than ourselves.

So get involved in something that makes your heart sing! This can be a volunteer activity or some other affiliation. There are many organizations, both non-profit and for profit, that are doing good work and that would love to have the benefit of your time and expertise. There are probably individuals in your world that are looking for your help (the little old lady down the street who needs transportation, your neighbor who is building an addition, the single mom who needs someone to help her with her child, etc.). You can make a big difference for people in seemingly small ways.

Use your knowledge, skills and abilities to do something for someone else. Do something that brings a smile to someone's face, puts a song in their heart and a dance to their feet. And remember that getting involved isn't about the other person—it's about you making a difference for yourself.

Exercises

Rent and watch "About a Boy". This is a humorous take on getting involved, albeit reluctantly, for big results.

Scan the local papers for local charity events looking for volunteers. When you find something of interest, join the cause.

Post your availability on the local coffee shop bulletin board. You never know who will cross your path with an interesting opportunity.

Watch the rhythm of your community. Do you see that there might be someone who could use your help? If yes, you know what to do.

Make a financial contribution to a non-profit organization serving a cause near and dear to your heart. Actually go to the organization and see where your contribution is making a difference. Ask to meet with recipients of their work to learn how donations have made a difference in the lives.

At day's end, consider how your involvement has changed someone else's world. Feel the energy you have as a result of giving—it might even be similar to that good muscle ache that you get after vigorous physical exercise. Journal your observations in how your active involvement changed both your outer and inner worlds.

Reflections

"You must get involved to have an impact. No one is impressed with the won-lost record of the referee."

~ *John H. Holcomb*

Reflections

"The difference between involvement and commitment is like ham and eggs. The chicken is involved; the pig is committed."

~ Martina Navratilova

Problem Solving

"Obstacles are those frightful things you see when you take your eyes off your goals."

~ Friedrich Wilhelm Nietzsche

Today is the final day of this program. If anything that remains outstanding as something to get handled, it's time to make that happen. Remember that every problem is an opportunity for you to choose your response and grow from it. What choice points and learning opportunities are waiting for you now? There are five steps to directly solving a problem.

1. Assess the situation: what are all the variables? What is really going on?
2. Identify the symptoms: what are all the signs that something is happening?
3. Look at the sources of those symptoms: what is underneath the symptoms?
4. Experience the shift of illumination: what is the greater message of the problem source?
5. Create a solution: through comprehensive understanding, a solution(s) can be created. Remember that a solution exists for every problem—always and every time.

Remember that the same mind that created the problem may not be able to solve the problem; it may be necessary to get outside help from a trusted friend or advisor. Asking for assistance is a sign of maturity and ability to receive; asking for help and being willing to accept it is more than just problem solving. It is the natural give and take of life, and the cycle of giving and receiving is one of the most basic natural rhythms we live by.

The size of a problem is relative; that is, the problem is larger when we feel less able to handle it. One person's problem may not even show up as an issue at all for someone else. Increase your capacity to handle problems by addressing yours—it is through the experience of getting through problems that we build our confidence and our capacity to handle our challenges. In fact, if we had no problems to solve, life would probably be pretty boring and we could be weak in character. In nature, we see that a tree's roots become stronger with big winds.

Use all of your knowledge, skills, attitudes and abilities to put what you have learned into action to problem solve any outstanding challenges for yourself (or others, for that matter!). Be in gratitude for the opportunity to grow, and be gentle with yourself through the process. It can take a lot of energy to solve problems—do what you need to do to support your well-being as you grow through addressing and mastering your challenges.

Exercises

Take an inventory of any challenges, issues or loose ends that need to be addressed. Follow the five step process in creating a customized solution, so that you can address it and move on. And when you do, celebrate the ending of that lesson!

Consider the last time you were faced with a daunting problem. How did you handle it? Could you have handled it better? Take note of your default problem solving patterns. Now having the five step problem solving process, could you have problem solved more quickly?

When thinking about your ability to problem solve, do you find negative emotions or thoughts come up to prevent your ability to be effective in your problem solving? If so, ask for a message about the underlying positive intention of that emotion or thought. Acknowledge and understand what is happening for you, then let it go. Replace it with a positive trust in your ability to be confident and effective in your problem solving ability.

Interview three people you admire about their problems. Ask them to define "problem", to share how they address their problems, and how they know they are successful in their problem solving. Learn from their process what you can do to be more effective in your problem solving.

Before going to sleep tonight, reflect on your day. Consider what problems you were able to solve today, and how your problem solving process has changed over time (for example, what problems used to feel big for you that now seem so simple). Write your feelings and thoughts about how mastering problems effectively affects your world.

Reflections

"Never bring the problem-solving stage into the decision- making stage. Otherwise, you surrender yourself to the problem rather than the solution."

~Robert Schuller

Reflections

*"We are all faced with a series of great opportunities
brilliantly disguised as unsolvable problems."*

~ John W. Gardner

Final Intention

For the past 33 years, I've looked in the mirror every morning and asked myself "If today were the last day of my life, would I want to do what I am about to do today?"

~ Steve Jobs, Apple founder

You have undertaken a significant rejuvenation and life creation journey for the past 21 days. You have confronted emotions, thoughts, patterns, habits, routines, and awareness to determine whether they serve you or not in living your best life. You have visualized, journaled, and felt your way to a new reality. You have created a new way of being by paying attention to whom you are now, today—and who you want to be. You have shown courage, commitment and clarity in your truths.

It is my most sincere intention for you that you will continue to stretch from the inside out on this journey of living your best life. Continue to rejuvenate on a regular basis... if and when you find your old ways creeping in, revisit this book. This book is all about you and it is yours to use it as much as you need it to experience your rejuvenated life on purpose.

Celebrate the completion of the last three weeks by doing something special for yourself. Feel the empowerment and confidence that comes from proactively defining your best life. Know that you get to choose to rejuvenate, create and change your life on a continuing daily basis.

I hope you continue this powerful journey of living your best life on purpose every day. May you be protected and cared for as you live your best life.

Warmly,

Inez

About the Author

I help people become their best, helping them to use their own definition of best and make their own choices to achieve that goal.

I've worked as a classroom teacher, drug abuse prevention counselor, social worker, and union advocate, all of which has given me a grounded approach in strategic planning, motivation, negotiation and leadership development. As a corporate executive, I've designed and delivered educational and human services programs personal esteem, diversity competency, team building, time management and conflict resolution.

I seek to live my best life by bringing my experience and skills to the task of understanding the vision, process, and commitment such a lifestyle requires.

I'm a lifelong learner who strives to be my best at living life to the fullest. After receiving an undergraduate degree in biology, I trained as a computer programmer and also completed a master's program in organizational development. I obtained life coach and group coaching certification, and studied at the Life Purpose Institute.

My company, The Bracy Group, Inc., is a leader in personal development training, career coaching, visioning, and speaking services for organizations and individuals ready to be their best. You can reach me at http://InezBracy.com.

My training and experience help me to help others find the same peace I seek, the serenity of a life lived to the fullest, a life where my rainbow guides and cheers me every day.

Made in the USA
Columbia, SC
06 February 2018